After-School
FUN

Gymnastics

by JoAnn Early Macken

Reading consultant: Susan Nations, M.Ed., author/literacy coach/consultant

WR WEEKLY READER
EARLY LEARNING LIBRARY

Please visit our web site at: www.earlyliteracy.cc
For a free color catalog describing Weekly Reader® Early Learning Library's list
of high-quality books, call 1-877-445-5824 (USA) or 1-800-387-3178 (Canada).
Weekly Reader® Early Learning Library's fax: (414) 336-0164.

Library of Congress Cataloging-in-Publication Data

Macken, JoAnn Early, 1953-
    Gymnastics / by JoAnn Early Macken.
       p. cm. — (After-school fun)
    Includes bibliographical references and index.
    ISBN 0-8368-4513-7 (lib. bdg.)
    ISBN 0-8368-4520-X (softcover)
    1. Gymnastics—Juvenile literature. I. Title.
    GV461.3.M32   2005
    796.44—dc22   2004059703

This edition first published in 2005 by
Weekly Reader® Early Learning Library
330 West Olive Street, Suite 100
Milwaukee, WI 53212 USA

Photographer: Gregg Andersen
Picture research: Diane Laska-Swanke
Art direction and page layout: Tammy West

Printed in the United States of America

1 2 3 4 5 6 7 8 9 09 08 07 06 05

Note to Educators and Parents

Reading is such an exciting adventure for young children! They are beginning to integrate their oral language skills with written language. To encourage children along the path to early literacy, books must be colorful, engaging, and interesting; they should invite the young reader to explore both the print and the pictures.

After-School Fun is a new series designed to help children read about the kinds of activities they enjoy in their free time. In each book, young readers learn about a different artistic endeavor, physical activity, or learning experience.

Each book is specially designed to support the young reader in the reading process. The familiar topics are appealing to young children and invite them to read — and reread — again and again. The full-color photographs and enhanced text further support the student during the reading process.

In addition to serving as wonderful picture books in schools, libraries, homes, and other places where children learn to love reading, these books are specifically intended to be read within an instructional guided reading group. This small group setting allows beginning readers to work with a fluent adult model as they make meaning from the text. After children develop fluency with the text and content, the book can be read independently. Children and adults alike will find these books supportive, engaging, and fun!

— Susan Nations, M.Ed., author, literacy coach,
and consultant in literacy development

After school, I go to gymnastics. I wear my leotard. I meet my friends in the gym.

5

First, we warm up.

We stretch our arms.

We stretch our legs.

We stretch our bodies.

We do our floor exercises. I am learning to do a cartwheel. My coach helps me balance.

My coach lifts me up on the uneven bars. Chalk helps keep my hands from slipping. I swing back and forth.

I like to watch
the other gymnasts.
The boys use other
equipment. My friend
holds himself up on the
parallel bars.

My friend practices on the pommel horse. His legs circle around. They cut back and forth like a scissors.

I practice running and jumping. I jump off a springboard. I land on a mat.

My older sister uses
the springboard, too.
She jumps over the
vaulting horse. Some
day, I will, too.

I walk on the balance beam. I balance on one foot. Gymnastics is hard work, but I like to practice. I like to feel strong.

Glossary

balance — to stay steady and stable by putting an equal amount of weight on each side of something

cartwheel — a sideways handspring with arms and legs out like a wheel

leotard — a stretchy suit worn for dancing and gymnastics

springboard — a flexible board used for jumping or diving

For More Information

Books

The Best Book of Gymnastics. Christine Morley (Kingfisher)

Cat on the Mat. Susan Schade (Random House)

D. W. Flips. Marc Brown (Little, Brown)

First Day at Gymnastics. Anita Ganeri (Dorling Kindersley)

Web Sites

Brown's Gymnastics Kid's Corner
www.brownsgym.com/resources/ kid_corner.htm
Gymnastics pictures to color, diagrams of positions, and activities

Index

About the Author

JoAnn Early Macken is the author of two rhyming picture books, *Sing-Along Song* and *Cats on Judy*, and six other series of nonfiction books for beginning readers. Her poems have appeared in several children's magazines. A graduate of the M.F.A. in Writing for Children and Young Adults program at Vermont College, she lives in Wisconsin with her husband and their two sons. Visit her Web site at www.joannmacken.com.